DOCKLA *LIGH*

Official Handbook

Alan Pearce
Stephen Jolly
Brian Hardy

Capital Transport

ISBN 185414 166 X

Published by Capital Transport Publishing
38 Long Elmes, Harrow Weald, Middlesex

Printed by Winchmore Press
Fowler Road, Hainault, Ilford, Essex

Photographic credits

Docklands Light Railway 14, 17,18, 21 centre, 25 right, 36, 49 lower, 50, 66, 67, 70, 73

Capital Transport Publishing 1, 2, 3, 12, 16 centre, 20, 21 top, 27, 28 centre, 30, 32, 33, 35, 38, 39, 42, 45, 46, 47 bottom, 48, 52, 53, 54 top, 55, 56, 57 centre and bottom, 58, 59 bottom, 60, 61, 62, 63, 64, 74, 77, front and back covers

Alan Blake 47 top and centre, 59 top

Brian Hardy 26, 34, 37, 43, 54 bottom, 57 top

London Transport 23, 28 bottom

Brian Morrison 4, 15

Alan Pearce 6, 9, 10, 11, 13, 16 top, 25 left, 31, 49 upper, 65

Contents

Introduction

The closure of London's up-river docks had left the capital with an area of about 8½ square miles suffering all the signs of urban dereliction; the jobs had gone or moved downstream to container handling ports like Tilbury, public transport had declined and social, retail and leisure facilities had either gone or had not kept pace with the type, quantity and quality appearing elsewhere in London.

Central Government's solution was to create in 1981 an urban development corporation — the LDDC — with the aim of achieving physical, economic and social regeneration of the area. The LDDC identified the need to provide permanent links to help attract and keep the confidence of commerce and industry.

In October 1982 — only four months after a report entitled 'Public Transport Provision for Docklands' had been submitted — the Government agreed to fund the building of what became the Docklands Light Railway as a project of regional and national importance. However, the project was only to go ahead under strictly controlled conditions and the outturn price was not to exceed £77m, to be funded jointly by the Department of Transport and the Department of the Environment via the GLC and the LDDC respectively. The railway was to open in 1987. Although advantage was to be taken of contemporary technology, technical solutions were not to be incorporated that could significantly increase the risk of cost-overrun or compromise the railway's completion date or reliable operation.

London Transport acting as agent for the joint clients the GLC and the LDDC was made responsible for managing the Parliamentary process, constructing the railway and opening it within the criteria set down by Government. Initially the strategy was to invite separate tenders for specific portions of the whole project. However, this was changed to a single-package tendering process with the commercial bidders forming multi-capable design, build and construct teams utilising what was available from the world Light Rail industry, or could be developed in time, to meet the client's Performance Specification. By this process, GEC-Mowlem, as a joint venture, was awarded the contract on 22nd August 1984 with a proposal which had evolved into an automatic, segregated, low-level power collection railway.

As construction pushed ahead, confidence in Docklands increased. Land that had once had a negative value (it costing more to demolish buildings standing on the land than the land itself was worth) rose towards half a million pounds per acre and beyond. Redevelopment schemes became grander and grander culminating in the simply massive Canary Wharf project first considered in 1985. Consisting of three tall tower blocks and a mass of other developments offering ten million square feet of office space, it was projected to be the base for 40,000 jobs. Clearly, the original DLR as then being built was no match for the transport demands of this scheme.

With the initial railway still under construction another Parliamentary Bill was deposited to seek powers to construct tunnels to an underground station at Bank, in the heart of the City. With the public opening in 1987 approaching, the contract to substantially upgrade the initial, open-air railway was placed with GEC-Mowlem so that when public service commenced on 31st August 1987 work was already underway for this upgrading. A contract with E.Nuttall Ltd for the tunnel to Bank had also been signed. By March 1988 tunnelling for the Bank extension had begun and although the original Leamouth-routed Beckton Extension Bill was delayed the same month in favour of a revised route via Canning Town, the DLR entered the 1990s with simultaneous construction projects to the west and the east. This substantial and at times disruptive upgrading work was carried out with an increasing working population expecting the original 1984 specification railway, with its mere 11 trains, to perform something close to perfection. To this complex situation was added the considerable lobbying by the boroughs of Lewisham and Greenwich, situated to the south of the River Thames, to have the DLR extended to their side of the river. This culminated in the Lewisham extension project, Parliamentary powers for which were gained in May 1993.

Planning the DLR

The DLR was not the first planned attempt to improve transport links in Docklands. London Transport had plans in the 1970s to extend the tube network eastwards, close to the River Thames. This line would have passed under the river a number of times. Already at that time estimated to cost £325m, it was its high cost that killed it off.

Also starting in the 1970s, London Transport had considered the use of Light Rail in several areas of London: Croydon to New Addington, Finsbury Park and Muswell Hill and between Hatton Cross and Terminal 4 at Heathrow Airport.

Once intentions were refocused on Docklands, various Light Rail options were drawn up before the final design was chosen. Within the plan for a north-south and an east-west line (which would not have provided a direct City to Isle of Dogs link) Mile End Underground station originally figured as the northern railhead. It was intended to have a street-based line running from the Limehouse area to Mile End along Burdett Road (the road later used by the Docklands Clipper bus and more recently figuring in plans for a Busway). Later, the Poplar to Bow railway line, as now used by the DLR, was to have been used with the line turning southwest at Bow to run along the Mile End Road to Mile End Underground station. The ultra-tight timescale imposed and the large number of authorities involved worked against both of these possibilities. There is today little doubt that the line to Stratford is a much more worthwhile one.

Until the era of the large-scale development proposals for the Isle of Dogs (from mid-1986 onwards), the DLR was expected to actually have to look for traffic and customers, rather than as has happened since, to have an embarrassment of business. Thus, the planning assumed relatively low hourly figures to move — 1,500 initially, per hour/per direction. This capacity level resulted in a planned timetable of eight departures per hour on each of the two legs of the Initial Railway, combining to give a more impressive 16 trains per hour serving the combined section of route on the Isle of Dogs. It was to meet this part of the Performance Specification that the tendering parties bid in 1984 and it was this simple timetable that the railway used for its pre-marketing. However, what had seemed attractive, and indeed almost too good to be true to some local residents in 1984, proved to be an embarrassment by the time the railway was actually ready to carry passengers a mere three years later.

Planning work to upgrade the system began before the public opening in 1987. Simply put, the planners required the railway to be rebuilt with a remodelled main junction at Poplar and with longer platforms to accept two-unit trains. The trains were to be run more frequently with an improved signalling system with more operational flexibility such as provided by reversing facilities at Crossharbour and a passing loop at Pudding Mill Lane. The railway company at the same time was required to run a passenger service to meet the expectations of the growing workforce and the local residents who had long been promised better public transport.

Now that the upgrading work is beginning to deliver a bigger railway, the capacity figures start to speak for themselves. Even with only a single track service to Bank, the hourly capacity between the City and the Isle of Dogs rose towards 6,000 people per hour/per direction. When combined with improvements to the Stratford and the City services, levels of capacity in excess of 10,000 per hour result on the Isle of Dogs leg as far south as Crossharbour, and 12,000 people per hour/per direction between the City and the junction north of the West India Docks. The planned-for addition of an under-river service to Lewisham will be providing an estimated 3,000 people per hour/per direction capacity in addition to the other flows.

The Docklands access picture will be dramatically improved by the planned 1998 opening of the Jubilee Line extension, bringing an hourly capacity of 22,000 passengers interchanging with the DLR at Canary Wharf and Canning Town.

By mid-decade, or about ten years after the original DLR took shape, many planning decisions will have been overturned, revised and remade. However it is worth remembering that several key features of the original schemes and plans remain.

These include the use of Light Rail technology, where appropriate, to climb severe gradients and take sharp curves, minimising landtake and potential intrusion. The original idea of a multi-stop, many stationed system remains, again developed out of Light Rail technology, even though some of those stations are now staffed sites. The railway remains as a locally managed distinct transport organisation, appropriate for a network serving a part of London unlike any other.

Opposite **The mock-up for the first batch of DLR vehicles is seen at the site of the design consultants W.S. Atkins, Epsom. It shows an early idea for the livery, with an anchor and chain link logo and orange stripes.**

Building the DLR

Although it may seem that the DLR was blessed with being able to use a lot of redundant railway land that no-one else had previously claimed, it was still necessary to establish relations with a great number of parties before construction could begin. In particular there were more than one hundred tenants trading from arches underneath the old viaduct on the City arm; at certain other places, notably south of Bow Church station and between Mudchute and Island Gardens other very sensitive property and occupation matters had to be tackled. Two-thirds of the 7.5 route miles (12.1 km) of the 1987 opening railway uses former disused or under-used railway. Some considerable new works, in volume and variety, were necessary to accommodate the DLR.

Starting at the City end, the original terminus at Tower Gateway is constructed on a reinforced concrete viaduct. A double track viaduct, since modified and rebuilt for the Bank extension, has been constructed eastwards parallel to the Railtrack-owned Fenchurch Street lines. In this area a reinforced concrete slab supported by the existing viaduct and independent foundations was constructed. Elsewhere an independent steel and concrete composite design has been used. At Cannon Street Road (1km east of Tower Gateway) the DLR joined the BR viaduct and adopted two original BR running rails.

At Shadwell the BR viaduct was used to carry the island platform structure. A 200 metre reinforced concrete viaduct was constructed south of Limehouse station (then called Stepney East) to avoid the existing BR running lines and to link into the western end of the disused brick arch viaduct of the former London & Blackwall Railway. From here to near to the north side of the West India Docks, the line used the 1839 constructed viaduct.

This structure was in remarkably good condition and though some arches required strengthening with a concrete overslab, others simply needed repointing. The 90 ft span at Limehouse Basin is a Grade II Listed Structure. In addition no fewer than 11 wrought iron bridge decks needed replacing with new concrete decks, although the old side girders were put back in to retain appearances. At West India Dock Road the two-span bridge was reconstructed to incorporate the original solid pink granite columns in the road. As originally built, the line rose up on to a standard steel and concrete composite structure leading to North Quay junction, originally built with 40-metre radius turnouts as part of three double junctions. South of this junction the Docks Crossing began. Specially fabricated 65-metre spans were provided in each of the three docks with an 8-metre clearance over the water of the dock. This structure, which in the mid-1980s dominated the skyline, is now dwarfed by the vast office buildings around it.

South of the West India Dock system, the line turns east on a 50-metre radius curve typical of Light Rail systems and then winds its way south through the island on standard elevated structure although a specially fabricated section was used to cross the Millwall Cut, the stretch of water connecting the West India and Millwall docks.

The construction of the viaducts of the original railway followed a simple steel beam and concrete deck pattern. Here the South Quay station structure is being assembled.

The West India Dock crossing required a longer span allowing a very graceful viaduct design to be used. Building work here is seen from South Quay work site with the Canary Wharf warehouses in the background.

Island Gardens station viaduct being constructed, showing the decorative brick arches.

South of Crossharbour the line uses an earth embankment before being carried on a new viaduct containing Mudchute station to join the 27 surviving arches of the single track Millwall Park viaduct. The southern end of the viaduct was raised to aid clearance over Manchester Road when the bridge was reinstated.

The route from North Quay junction to Poplar and Stratford was built with several one-off features. The bridge over what was the Docklands Northern Relief Road, now Aspen Way, is a 50 metre span skew plate girder bridge. Poplar station was originally built on retained-fill immediately southwest of the Operations and Maintenance Centre. The old trackbed was re-ballasted and new drainage provided north of Poplar. A steel plate girder bridge was needed to cross the Limehouse Cut Canal south of Devons Road because the earlier structure had decayed badly.

North of Bow the Bow Curve takes the line from the old cutting to run beside British Rail on an embankment featuring a 1 in 25 gradient on a 100 metre radius curve. New ballasted track was laid towards Stratford on the alignment of the most southerly of the BR lines and only minimal engineering work was needed to adapt the western end bay platform for DLR trains to use.

North Quay Junction east side with track installation underway.

Harbour Exchange curve during the installation of the reinforced concrete track foundation panels.

The viaduct across Regents Canal at Limehouse is a listed structure and has been adapted carefully to carry City-bound trains.

Westferry station from the south during construction, with the DLR publicity minibus alongside.

The City extension

The Initial Railway had been constructed under a design and build contract with GEC-Mowlem Railway Group carrying out all the tasks necessary to provide a complete railway.

This formula was repeated with the extension further into the City, to Bank Station. On 17th July 1987 — before the original railway had even opened for traffic — two contracts were awarded; to Edmund Nuttall Ltd, for the westward extension in tunnel to Bank, including construction of the DLR station at Bank; and to GEC-Mowlem Railway Group, for the upgrading of the existing system, extension of electrical systems through the E.Nuttall contract works, and provision of new vehicles.

A single 100-tonne tunnelling machine was constructed in Britain, to a German design, to bore the 1.6 km extension westwards from Royal Mint Street. Following a Start of Tunnelling ceremony on 14th March 1988 the westbound tunnel was bored first, breaking through into the new King William Street station site on 7th December 1988. The machine was then withdrawn from the westbound tunnel and put to work digging the second one, to become the eastbound tunnel. This bore was completed in February 1990. Tunnelling through the London clay was achieved at an average rate of nearly 100 metres per week.

Right **Inside the westbound running tunnel of the extension to Bank, showing the emergency walkway on the left.**

Below **The route of the City extension.**

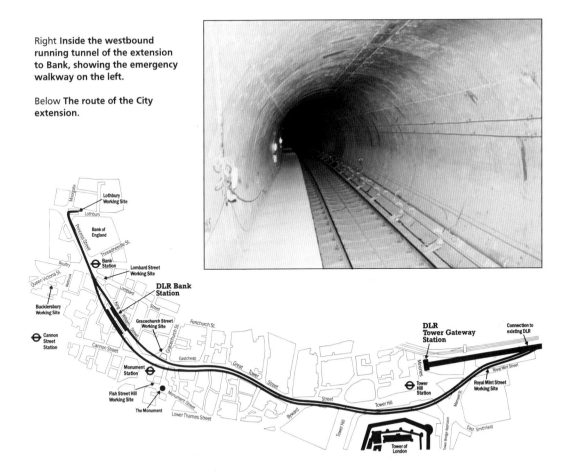

The circular cross section tunnels were bored by the 5.39 metre diameter tunnelling machine, then lined with precast concrete segmental linings: the internal tunnel diameter is five metres. This tunnel diameter permits the provision of a walkway on one side, which allows not only access for maintenance but evacuation of passengers, including mobility-impaired passengers, in an emergency. In order to bore the larger seven-metre station tunnels the existing tunnelling machine was plugged into the centre of a larger 7.75 metre station tunnel machine, retaining the smaller machine's facilities to power the larger machine. As much as 200,000 tonnes of clay was excavated and taken to various sites east of London including the site of the former Beckton Gasworks. Generally, the tunnels were bored at depths greater than 30 metres below ground with the Bank station at a depth up to 42 metres below ground.

Besides the tunnelling carried out by machine, ventilation shafts, access points, escalator shafts and interconnecting tunnels were dug by the traditional hand method. In order to minimise surface impact, available space on street corners was used for worksites: as well as the main contract site at Royal Mint Street beside the DLR, four other worksites were used at Fish Street Hill, Lombard Street, Lothbury and Bucklersbury.

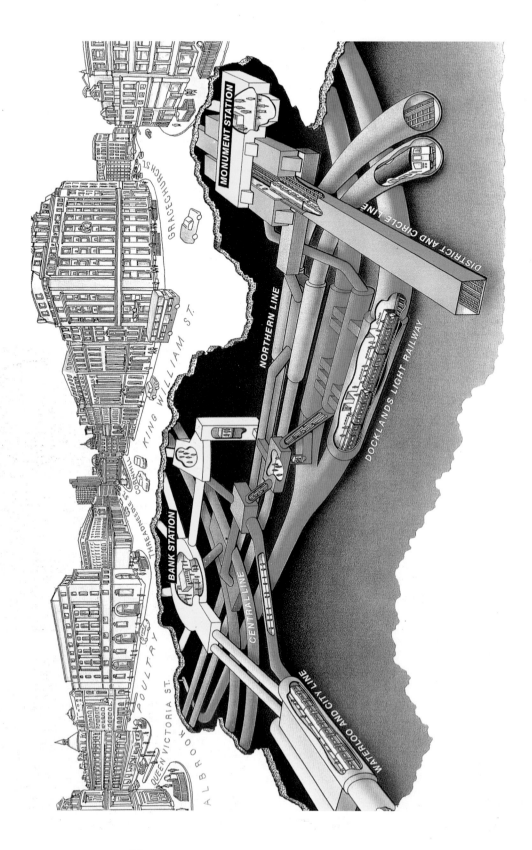

Beneath the Mansion House, a Grade 1 listed building, it was necessary to dig a step-plate junction which is a series of expanding tunnel diameters to accommodate a rail junction between the two running lines. Special tie bars were used to secure Mansion House following the necessary approvals in July 1990. The step-plate junction was completed in March 1991 and although there were some signs of movement in one corner of the building, it suffered no damage.

As well as the main work, substantial effort was needed to rebuild and integrate the London Underground Monument station to provide links to the new DLR facilities. In particular a new concrete slab was cast above the existing station to support a new building to be constructed over the ticket hall. This required 30 metres deep hand-dug shafts to accommodate the necessary vertical piles.

The first DLR train into Bank was P86 vehicle 03 hauled by a diesel locomotive and used for measurement purposes on 11th July 1990; slightly over one year later, public opening using the westbound tunnel was achieved on 29th July 1991 with the second eastbound tunnel following on 29th November 1991.

Opposite **The relationship of the DLR tunnels to the other railway tunnels in the Bank area. A long overrun tunnel from the DLR platforms allows a failed train to be removed without disrupting traffic.**

Below **A DLR train at Bank in March 1991, four months before services commenced.**

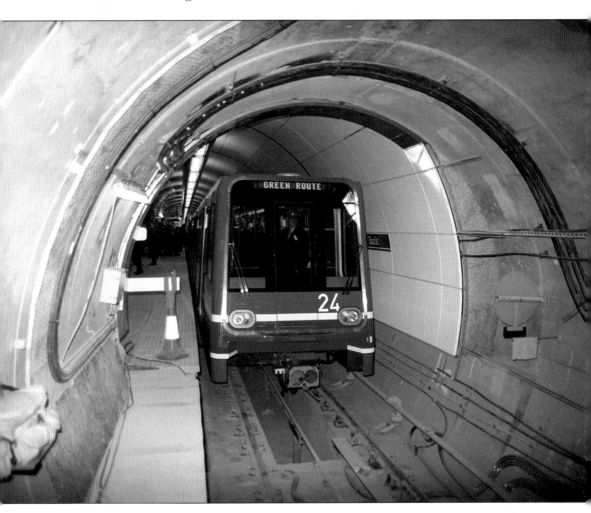

The upgrading contract

The original American-backed and later Canadian-based developers Olympia & York envisaged Canary Wharf as, in effect, a third city centre within London, complementing the City and the West End. In the roundest of terms Canary Wharf's population suggested a staggering 250 per cent growth in DLR traffic forecasts. In reality, even without Canary Wharf's population in place, the DLR still experienced loadings of 34,000 passengers per day (against a 22,000 figure computed from the original Performance Specification hourly flow figures) some two years after opening. These figures were achieved in spite of evening and weekend closures imposed by engineering upgrading work.

At the same time as the decision-making process gave the go-ahead for the physical extension of the railway to Bank, a decision was taken to upgrade the rest of the railway to handle more passengers.

The upgrading work divided into five main parts: the strengthening of structures, where necessary, to run two-unit trains, lengthening platforms to handle these longer trains; infrastructure improvements to aid operational flexibility; buying more trains; and specific upgrading work such as the total rebuilding of Canary Wharf station.

Above **The north side viaduct of the remodelled delta junction at Poplar.**

It may seem difficult to appreciate now, but until the advent of the Canary Wharf scheme for the Isle of Dogs it was intended that the main DLR service would be from the City to Beckton with the Isle of Dogs to be served by the north-south service from Stratford, passengers changing at Poplar between one route and the other.

In order to allow the upgrading work to be completed as quickly as possible it was necessary to grant the contractor, GEC-Mowlem, possession of the railway in the evenings, overnight and at weekends. Essential though this was, immediately after the railway opened in 1987, weekend traffic, especially on the Saturday and Sunday afternoons, was particularly buoyant. To cover the periods of shutdown, replacement bus services have been operated, serving station to station bus stops at the nearest convenient point to the DLR and conforming to the Isle of Dogs–Tower Gateway and Isle of Dogs–Stratford pattern.

It is true to say that most of the worst disruptions associated with the upgrading contract are now over. In December 1990 the platform extensions at eight stations were commissioned for two-unit trains, these being West India Quay, Heron Quays, South Quay and Crossharbour on the Island and Tower Gateway, Shadwell, Limehouse and Westferry on the City leg. In January 1991 Poplar, All Saints, Devons Road and Bow Church followed suit.

Work has been completed under a separate contract to extend platforms at Mudchute and Island Gardens to permit two-car trains to operate south of Crossharbour. This has increased capacity to the southern extremity of the existing system.

Improvements to the infrastructure of the railway to improve operational flexibility have included the construction of a passing loop at Pudding Mill Lane on the long single track section from south of Bow Curve to Stratford. This was commissioned on 21st May 1990.

At Crossharbour the southbound line was diverted from 27th February 1989 to allow for the construction of a centre siding to permit City trains to reverse after having served the principal traffic generators on the Isle of Dogs at Canary Wharf, South Quay and Crossharbour. This new siding was available from 1st November 1990.

Relatively minor but still useful improvements have been carried out at Tower Gateway. On 24th September 1990 an additional flight of stairs was opened beside the existing pair of escalators and staircase and on 3rd December 1990 an eastern exit from the end of the single island platform was opened to provide relief for what had become a heavily congested platform. Staff control of passenger flows on to the platform, synchronised with train arrivals, unloading and departure sequences, had previously become necessary.

The most spectacular upgrading work has taken place at Canary Wharf to produce a station appropriate to the scale of the surrounding development. Instead of two side platforms serving a pair of tracks, a four track station with six platform faces has been built. Like Tower Gateway and Bank, Canary Wharf is served by escalators. These serve four of the six platforms (platforms 2/3 southbound and 4/5 northbound) but not the outer side platforms (platforms 1 and 6).

As rebuilt, the station now opens via platforms 1 and 6 onto the upper retailing level of the Canary Wharf development and a broad station concourse below merges into the lower level retail developments. The platforms are covered by an impressive all-over steel arch roof.

The original bridge structure has been changed — effectively doubled in width — to accommodate a three-track layout in plan form at this station, although a four-track facility has been extended northwards through the rebuilt West India Quay station. The southbound running line was diverted onto the most easterly of the flow trackbeds on 21st May 1990, followed by the diversion of the northbound line on to the western side of the widened bridge structure on 18th June 1990.

Less than one year later, on 2nd April 1991, the Canary Wharf station was opened for contractors' use and just over four months later on 12th August 1991, the station opened to the public using the outer two tracks and corresponding side platforms (platforms 1 and 6). Then on 9th December 1991 the two island platforms (with four faces: platforms 2 to 5 inclusive) together with their four escalators were opened.

Opposite **Canary Wharf station, in the middle of the office development, provides a dramatic contrast with Heron Quays to the south of it. Heron Quays like most of the other stations of the original DLR has had its platforms extended to take longer trains but is otherwise largely as built. To the north of Canary Wharf is the upgraded West India Quay station and the flying junctions of the North Quay area.**

The Beckton extension

The Beckton extension consists of three main contracts. To the west is a 2 km contract awarded to Balfour Beatty to build the complex of viaducts and interchanges where the Beckton line separates from the existing railway at North Quay and Poplar. The larger contract for 8.5km of railway and valued at £116m has been built by the joint venture company Mowlem/Taylor Woodrow. A contract with BN Belgium provided for new rolling stock, initially for 34 but later increased with an order for a further 26.

The western end contract involved three main tasks: to replace the existing three-way junction with a grade-separated interchange; to upgrade Poplar station from three to four tracks and to construct a 1,650-tonne new bridge over the Limehouse Link road.

The main Beckton contract consists of approximately one-third each of elevated, ground level and trough or underpass-level railway. Concrete structures which are more expensive but more substantial than the earlier steel/concrete composite design are used throughout for the elevated portions, which are located principally in the Poplar to Leamouth/Brunswick areas, at the Connaught Crossing viaduct and near Gallions Reach station.

Where the DLR crosses the River Lea a post-tensioned box girder bridge with a 74-metre span has been erected. Further east, the track descends to ground level but two stations, Beckton Park and Cyprus, were constructed in the centre of the Royal Albert Dock spine road as part of that contract. The track is also located within an underpass near the eastern end of the route in order to pass under the Eastern Gateway access road which is the main link road to the A406 North Circular Road.

The Beckton line at the eastern end of Poplar depot with the eastbound viaduct flying over the Stratford line tracks.

Although no powers are currently being sought for eastwards extensions beyond Beckton, various plans have been prepared at different dates to extend the railway to Barking (north east of Beckton) or towards Dagenham (due east of Beckton). Such proposals depend upon a further round of investment confidence developing in Docklands, as well as on plans affecting the Thames corridor. The confirmed route and the number of Thames-side stations on the Channel Tunnel high-speed rail link (CTRL) may have some bearing on the future pattern of riverside developments east of the DLR. It should also be kept in mind that any services extended beyond Beckton will be adding yet more stops to what will already be a 15-plus stopping service from the Beckton area to the City, on a railway serving Docklands and not designed to provide a fast link between essentially outer suburbs and central London. Nevertheless eastern extensions are not ruled out.

Top **The highest structure on the Beckton line is at the Connaught crossing of the Royal Docks and is designed as a future possible station site.**

Above **One of the 'bowl' stations under construction towards the eastern end of the Beckton extension.**

Publicity for the Beckton extension inside a DLR train.

Below While work was being undertaken in Beckton Depot, 21 B stock units had to be stored on the route of the Beckton extension in June and July 1993. These were formed into one long train, seen on the East India viaduct.

The Lewisham extension

This planned extension would join the existing railway north of Mudchute station, with a replacement station to be built north of the present Mudchute stop. It would then go underground on the north side of the current Millwall Park alignment with a new sub-surface Island Gardens station to be constructed north of the present terminus station, which would be demolished. The tunnels would go under the River Thames with an underground station, called Cutty Sark, proposed to be built between Thames Street and Creek Road.

The line would then curve south westwards to surface near the existing Greenwich station, continuing as an elevated railway along the alignment of Deptford Creek. A station is proposed for south of Deptford Bridge with the route then continuing principally through existing open space towards a stop at Elverson Road, proceeding to the west of Conington Road to terminate at an elevated station south of the existing Lewisham station ticket hall.

Originally floated as an idea by the London Borough of Lewisham after a brief engineering feasibility study had been conducted, this proposal was as dramatic as the decision to tunnel an extension to Bank. Although there is no fundamental difference between tunnelling under City buildings and under the River Thames, the engineering impact on the DLR would not be inconsiderable. A southward extension will also introduce new traffic flows from south east London into the DLR planning regime.

DLR Greenwich station is proposed to be fitted into the present railway layout at Greenwich by moving the present westbound railway track (left side) towards the eastbound one (right side) and fitting DLR into the resulting space. The DLR station will be towards the far end of the railway station as seen in this view.

DLR trains

On any railway, the trains present the most important element of a passenger's journey. It is now generally recognised that a train is not solely a functional piece of hardware, but an essential part of the image both in external appearance and the internal finish and comfort. This was realised by the railways' joint clients and by the contractor, and substantial efforts were made to ensure high standards of engineering and finish.

Not only does the train need to react to the elements of the signalling system to ensure a safe, timely and accurate passage from one station to the next, there is also the requirement for the train to communicate status changes, such as passenger alarm operations or the change of mode of driving (e.g. from 'automatic' to 'manual'). The car doors, control panels, power circuits and braking systems all have direct communication links with the 'outside world' of signalling commands, in addition to the internal connections normally found. With all this in mind, it is clearly not practicable to simply buy a train ready made 'off the shelf', put it on the rails and expect it to function. Thus, more than ever before, the rolling stock has to be seen as an integral part of the whole system.

Light Rail Vehicles (LRVs) are produced in quantity in Germany, France and Italy and West German technology in particular is exported across the world, notably to North America where, like Britain, the lack of a domestic market has for years inhibited the development of a home-based LRV product. The contractors for the DLR were thus faced with either opting for overseas designs or starting from scratch in Britain. In the context of the DLR (in its initial form) evolving a whole new design for just 11 cars could not be justified. Main contractor GEC-Mowlem therefore co-operated with Linke Hofmann Busch (LHB), one of Germany's main builders of railway vehicles.

Under the agreement reached, LHB were to be responsible for the shell and bogies, whilst GEC would fit all electrical components in Britain. In the event, a sub-contract to have the interiors fitted out by one of Britain's leading builders failed to materialise and the cars

Below left The 'A' end of vehicle 03 being delivered to Poplar and about to be placed on British rails for the first time. This vehicle was the only P86 to be delivered without the Docklands logo already applied.

were completed at LHB's Saltzgitter works, with the first one rolled out with some ceremony on 20th June 1986. The eleven vehicles of what became known as 'P86' stock, were delivered by road and sea via Hamburg and King's Lynn from August 1986, the first car (01) arriving at Poplar on 7th August 1986. Each train comprises an 'A' end and a 'B' end, the latter being the end on which the Automatic Train Protection equipment is located. The last car of the first batch, No.11, was to make history several times. It was delivered direct to Debdale Park, Manchester on 9th February 1987 as the key part of a light rail demonstration where it became the first revenue-earning DLR car. The car was modified to accept a pantograph for the overhead power collection system installed by Balfour Beatty, a conversion which was remarkably simple involving little more than an additional roof member and a length of conduit to carry the main power cables down to its underframe. Car 11 was delivered to the DLR at Poplar on 30th March 1987 after the completion of the light rail demonstration. Car 11's main claim to fame, however, was to be on 30th July 1987 when, in the hands of Train Captain Gary Bonini, it carried Her Majesty the Queen and His Royal Highness the Duke of Edinburgh from Island Gardens to Poplar, and thence to Tower Gateway, on the occasion of the Royal Opening of the railway.

Above right The last vehicle of the P86 batch, No.11, performed a number of honours. Before arriving with the DLR it worked on the GMPTE test track at Debdale Park, Manchester in February/March 1987, being temporarily fitted with a pantograph for overhead current collection. Vehicle 11 was also used in the Royal opening ceremony on 30th July 1987, and was the first to be transferred to Essen in November 1991.

The P86 stock trains were always operated singly and were banned from operating on the tunnel section to Bank. Unit 06 arrives at South Quay heading for Island Gardens.

As mentioned earlier, great care was taken with both the interior and exterior design of the cars. Having a seating capacity of 84, they were mostly arranged in transverse bays of four — always popular on the Underground and elsewhere — to take full advantage of the large windows offering fine rooftop views of the changing Docklands scene. Nowhere is this more true than in the end seats, giving front seat passengers an almost unprecedented driver's eye view. Understandably, these seats are almost always the first to fill. There is, however, an emergency driving console for the Train Captain in the centre of the screen, locked when not in use. To increase circulation space, 12 longitudinal seats are provided in the centre section of the train, along with two wheelchair bays. The railway has some regular wheelchair users, but the bays are most heavily used by shoppers with wheeled trolleys and baby buggies, taking advantage of the railway's superb roll-on/roll-off facilities. In order to achieve good access for unassisted wheelchair users the cars have been designed to have a level car floor to platform gap of only 75 mm (about 3 inches). This ruled out conventional exterior plug doors and led to the adoption of inward-opening ('bat wing') swing plug doors. These were never an ideal solution but with the traffic levels then forecast at the time the contract was awarded, it was anticipated that the layout would be acceptable. However, the enormous upturn in development on the Isle of Dogs has put this aspect in a different perspective, and with future orders of rolling stock it has been necessary to have an alternative arrangement.

The initial fleet of eleven cars was supplemented by a further ten — the P89 stock — to increase the capacity of the Initial Railway and for the first phase of services underground to Bank. These cars were very similar to the first (P86) batch with only detailed modifications — mostly under the skin — made in the light of operational experience, the need for longer (two-unit) trains, and to enable them to operate underground to Bank. P86 cars are prohibited for underground running, as they do not meet tunnel running safety requirements.

The additional ten cars were ordered as part of the upgrading contract in July 1987 and different from the initial cars in that they were constructed in the UK. During 1986 BREL decided to enter the light rail market and entered a co-operative agreement with LHB, whose products are largely complementary to those of the UK builder. The DLR cars were the first products of this development, being subcontracted from GEC-Mowlem Railway Group to BREL York. Numbered in the series 12-21, the first vehicle (No.12) was delivered by road, arriving at Poplar on 12th December 1989, the last one (No.21) on 4th May 1990. After commissioning and trials, the first to enter service (No.12) did so on 11th May 1990.

The only cosmetic difference between the P89 cars as built and the first batch was in the destination displays. On the new cars these were in the form of 'Voltron' dot matrix displays, which were far more reliable than the originals on the P86 cars. On these, many had succumbed to having hand-operated swivelling destination boxes but

Two-unit operation of DLR trains commenced on 25th February 1991, although it was to be some time before most trains (of P89 and B90 stock) were so formed. Two coupled P89 units are seen at Bow Church, showing the new 'Docklands Light Rail' logo.

in May 1990 unit 01 was fitted with 'Voltron' destination displays and the whole P86 fleet was subsequently so converted. Other changed features included the fitting of bulbous panels by the inward opening doors to both the P86 and P89 trains, in an attempt to discourage passengers from standing in that area, and blue tinted fluorescent lights at the 'driving' ends to reduce reflection for Train Captains when driving manually in the darkened conditions. From 15th June 1991, trains appeared in service with 'Light Rail' roundels applied to the front ends and the centre sides of each section. Irrespective of their similarity, the P86 and P89 types are unable to operate together in two-unit trains as was first intended.

Right **P86 interior, showing the red bulbous panels which had to be fitted to the door areas to discourage standing passengers here.**

Below **Revised logos prepared during the period of London Transport control. The Light Rail roundel was added to trains in 1991 and removed following takeover of the DLR by the LDDC the following year. Neither of the styles illustrated appeared in service.**

The main features of the two batches of two-bodied articulated units of P86/89 stock vehicles can be summarised as follows:

GENERAL

Length:	28m	(91ft 10in)
Width:	2.65m	(8ft 8in)
Height:	3.40m	(1ft 2in)
Weight:	39 tonnes (38.4 tons) approx (tare)	
Bogie centres:	10m	(32ft 10in)
Bogie wheelbase:	2.10m	(6ft 11in)
Min track curve radius:	40m	(130ft)
Seating capacity:	84 (72 transverse, 12 longitudinal)	
Total capacity:	210 with normal standing load or 260 with crush load	
Maximum design speed:	80km/h (50 mph)	

BODY
– Steel construction with polyurethane painted finish.
– Four doorways each side per car, each of 1,300mm clear opening, fitted double inward-gliding doors, electro-pneumatically operated passenger control of door opening.
– Glass reinforced plastic framed seats with moquette covered cushions and squabs.

BOGIES
– Of welded H-frame construction, with rolling rubber ring primary and airbag secondary suspension. Roller bearing slewing rings. The outer bogies are motor, the longitudinal frame-mounted motor driving both axles via right angle gearboxes and flexible drives.
– Single disc brake per axle, the actuators on the motored bogies incorporating spring applied parking brakes.
– Resilient wheels of 740mm (2ft 5in) diameter new, 660mm (2ft 2in) minimum.

TRACTION CONTROL
– Supply: 750V dc from an under-running third rail.
– The two motors are fed in parallel from a two-phase chopper, giving an overall frequency of 528Hz. Each half of the chopper uses a single Gate Turn-off Thyristor (GTO).
– Maximum accelerating current: 700 amps/vehicle.

AUXILIARIES
– 24V battery charged by dc-dc converter.
– Compressor: Hydrovane (rotary vane) type TB11/C14.
– Couplers, automatic by Scharfenberg. (P86 are 96 pin, P89 are 128 pin).

PERFORMANCE DATA

Acceleration:	$1.0m/s^2$
Service braking:	$0.8m/s^2$
Emergency braking:	$1.2m/s^2$

Prior to the building of the B90 stock local residents and representatives of passengers' groups were invited to test and comment on the design by means of a full-size mock-up of one section.

It was originally envisaged that the P89 stock would provide the stock required for the Bank extension, but the unprecedented increases in passenger traffic and the authorised extension to Beckton highlighted the need for even more trains, and to operate double length (two-unit) trains wherever possible. A contract was subsequently awarded to BN Constructions Ferrovaires et Metalliques of Bruges in Belgium, initially for ten more trains of what became known as B90 stock. This would have given a total of 31 vehicles in the DLR fleet (11xP86, 10xP89 and 10xB90), but the BN order was subsequently increased to 21 vehicles (11xP86, 10xP89 and 21xB90; total 42). A mock-up of the new BN stock was made available for public inspection in late September/early October 1989, by which time the requirement for additional stock from BN had grown to 44 trains (11xP86, 10xP89 and 44xB90; total 65).

Perhaps the most noticeable feature of the B stock is its sliding doors, provided to improve boarding and alighting at stations, necessary because of the far greater use of the DLR than was originally envisaged. These doors, outside-mounted, form part of the loading gauge and the width of the main vehicle body is thus fractionally less than the P stock. Other different features include fewer transverse seats (allowing a greater standing capacity within the train), a front opening door allowing access between coupled units (superfluous apart from in emergency situations, since there are no foot plates over the couplers between units, and in the Bank tunnels in an emergency, access and detrainment is via the side doors onto

specially provided side tunnel platform walkways). The front seats for forward viewing remain, however, although the emergency driving console for the Train Captain has had to be 'split' into two sections, one on each side of the front door. The door operating panel for the Train Captain is located down the left hand side of the double doorway positions, rather than over the doorways as on the P stock and conventionally upholstered seats replace inset moquette panels used hitherto. All of the electronic equipment is located in a single locked interior cabinet, rather than in several different positions.

The final order for B stock comprises 70 trains, divided into two sub types — 23 units of B90 stock (numbered 22-44) and 47 units of B92 stock (45-91). The first train of B90 stock arrived via Dartford Docks at Poplar on 31st January 1991 and was available for test running and crew training from 23rd April. The last unit arrived on 27th September. The first train to enter service (unit 22) did so on 1st July 1991. These trains, like the P89 stock, are able to operate singly or two coupled together, but the two types are not operationally compatible. Four trains (22,24-26) were delivered with continental style vehicle numbers, but the rest were delivered with numbers in the New Johnston style — the first four were later altered to be identical. 'Light Rail' roundels were to be fitted to B90 units, but only 14 B90 trains received them. The others were not given roundels due to the impending announcement that the DLR would be taken over by the London Docklands Development Corporation. This happened from 1st April 1992.

The B90 and B92 stock was built by BN at Brugge in Belgium, where a B90 unit is seen under construction at the company's workshop, courtesy of whom this photograph was taken.

Included in the first 23 B90 units was one (No.35) which was fitted from the start with Alcatel equipment for testing purposes — a section of track in the Poplar area was set aside for testing purposes from 9th September 1991. Joining unit 35, the first two Alcatel-equipped B92 trains proper arrived at Poplar in October 1991, to give three units for testing. All of the others have been delivered direct to Beckton depot, being equipped from the start with the new Alcatel equipment. The first of these arrived on 10th March 1992 and testing was due to commence on the new extension soon after delivery, between Prince Regent and Beckton. Details of the B stock can be summarised as follows:

Length:	28m
Length over coupler:	28.8m
Width over doors:	2.65m
Body width:	2.50m
Overall height:	3.468m
Weight:	36 tonnes approx (tare)
Seating capacity:	70 (12 transverse pairs, 42 longitudinal, 4 tip-up)
Total capacity:	284 (6 passengers/sq m)
Maximum speed:	80km/h (50mph)
Bogies:	2 BN monomotor bogies, 1 BN trailer bogie
Traction:	Brush Electrical Machines
ATO/ATP:	Westinghouse (ATO), GEC (ATP) for 22 trains, Alcatel of Canada for 48 trains. (As delivered to DLR)
Wheels:	Resilient wheels of 740mm diameter new, 660mm min.
Min track curve:	38m

The first batch of DLR stock — the P86 — was not allowed to carry passengers on the Bank extension, as it was not designed with the necessary safety features for tunnel operation. Options considered included 'upgrading' the trains to make them suitable for tunnel work, to scrap them, or to find a buyer. In fact all eleven trains have been purchased by Essen Verkehrs AG of Essen for further service and with their new owners are being fitted with pantographs and cabs. The first unit to leave the DLR for its new owner was unit 11 on 14th November 1991, followed by unit 03 on 26th November. Unit 06 was transferred in July 1992. Unit 08 left DLR on 24th December 1993 closely followed by 02 on 29th December 1993. The remaining six units will stay at DLR until the resignalling changeover by agreement with EVAG.

In the meantime consideration was given to replacing the 'bat wing' doors on the P89 stock, to make access easier. P89 units 15 and 18 were involved in a collision at West India Quay delta junction on 22nd April 1991, causing damage to the 'A' end of 18 and the 'B' end of 15. BREL at Derby were awarded the contract to repair the damaged portions and also to do the alterations to the passenger doors — this train was the ideal prototype. A serviceable train was formed of the undamaged ends of 15A and 18B and was renumbered unit '18' (the identification is taken by the 'B' end, having the ATO/ATP equipment), re-entering service on 30th July 1991. The

The interior of a modified P89 stock vehicle shows the additional window necessary at the door slide-back positions, along with the re-arranged longitudinal seat pairs.

two damaged portions were moved by road to Derby at the end of May 1991, to become (renumbered) unit 15. It was decided that single-leaf doors would replace the inward folding doors, but because the vehicles were already built to maximum loading gauge, they could not be fitted outside the body shell as on the B stock. Therefore the doors had to slide back into specially constructed pockets, which meant some interior seating alterations. No seats were lost, but the transverse pair by the draught screen at each new pocket position was turned to become longitudinal. Door controls by the door sides as on B stock were fitted, as were door-close warbler tones. The bulbous panels by the doors were removed as they were no longer needed. The repaired and converted train, with New Johnston numbers but no Light Rail roundels, arrived back at Poplar on 18th December 1991, re-entering service in its new form on 27th February 1992. Conversion work was completed by August 1992. The DLR rolling stock will ultimately comprise 70 B stock (23 B90 and 47 B92) and ten P89 stock trains. It remains to be seen whether the ten (and, of course, non-standard) P89 trains will later be converted with Alcatel signalling equipment or whether they too will be disposed of and possibly more B stock built. The determining factor is catering for rising traffic and the timing of Lewisham extension. Work began in November 1993 in converting the B90 stock to Alcatel signalling, with unit 22 being the first.

A view of the sliding doors as fitted to P89 stock. A new window section has been fitted at the slide-back position underneath which are slots for ventilation. The modification did not cause a loss of passenger seats, but necessitated some being refitted in the longitudinal position. This view shows a new train indicator in place on the platform but not yet commissioned, above the type provided from when the line opened in 1987.

The routes described

Above The Beckton line viaduct crosses the twisty Bow Creek, where the River Lea joins the Thames, to take the railway from Poplar to Canning Town.

As opened in 1987 the DLR consisted of three legs meeting at a triangular junction located at the northern end of the Isle of Dogs. One leg ran westwards to the City (initially to Tower Gateway near Tower Bridge, now also to an underground station at Bank), one to Stratford to the north east and one to Island Gardens, the terminus at the southern end of the Isle of Dogs peninsular facing Greenwich and the Cutty Sark preserved sailing ship. The Beckton extension adds a fourth leg to the original Poplar junction area, which has been extensively rebuilt and enlarged. The planned Lewisham extension will extend the Isle of Dogs leg further south, under the River Thames to Greenwich and Lewisham, and portions of this route can be inspected from public spaces.

The City route

The DLR has two termini in the City of London: Bank underground station and the original elevated terminus called Tower Gateway.

Bank station, consisting of the two side-platform tunnels bored either side of a central concourse, is located below the other existing railway tunnels at Bank. Interchange via new and existing escalators and passageways is provided to the Central, Northern, Circle, District and Waterloo & City lines of London Underground.

Eastwards from the Bank platforms, twin 5 metre diameter bored tunnels proceed and are generally underneath existing surface streets rather than buildings. The tunnels follow the alignment of King William Street towards the Monument Underground station road junction, thence under Great Tower Street, under Tower Hill between the Tower Hill ticket hall concourse of the Underground station and the Tower of London, crossing underneath Mansell Street to emerge on the north side of Royal Mint Street, climbing up above ground to join the elevated DLR structure of the original DLR Tower Gateway — Shadwell section.

The Tower Gateway terminus is built on a new structure close to the eastern end of the Fenchurch Street platforms. The DLR station is on the east side of the street called Minories, under which a public subway provides a pedestrian link to Tower Hill Underground station.

To reach the Bank terminus, the line descends a 6 per cent gradient from the original viaduct on the left.

From Tower Gateway the new double track structure with a portion already substantially rebuilt near the Royal Mint Street/Leman Street road junction to incorporate the Bank extension junction trackwork, takes the line east as far as Cannon Street Road. Between here and Stepney the DLR tracks move slightly northwards on to the existing viaduct where British Rail relinquished the two most southerly of its Fenchurch Street lines. An island platform station is located at Shadwell where the east-west viaduct crosses Watney Street. The remains of the adjacent London & Blackwall station platform would have left insufficient room for the other outside platform had it been re-used. Interchange with the East London line of London Underground is provided via Watney Street and Cable Street.

Approaching Limehouse, a new structure is provided to carry the line over Butcher Row with a DLR station located east of Butcher Row allowing interchange between the Fenchurch Street line services and the DLR.

Limehouse station is built alongside the platforms used by BR services. Interchange is at street level.

East of this station the DLR line leaves the British Rail alignment and follows the course of the London & Blackwall Railway on the 1840 built brick arch viaduct abandoned by British Railways in 1962.

It is at this point that the first signs of the contemporary Docklands area scene emerge; major construction work to the south of the DLR in the former Regents Canal dock — also called Limehouse Basin — has produced the Limehouse Link road in tunnel under Limehouse. In the middle distance can be seen the new flats near the River Thames along Narrow Street and then the spectacular Canary Wharf development rises up from the old docks on the Isle of Dogs. The line continues eastward on the former London & Blackwall brick arch viaduct crossing Westferry Road, where another station, called Westferry, is located. Then, after crossing the West India Dock Road, the dramatic and at first sight complicated junctions at North Quay are reached. Simply put, as now remodelled, there is provision for the City services to run into the junction and southwards on to the Isle of Dogs with the Beckton services separated away on to the Beckton Link viaduct. Trains from Stratford will continue to share the same junction north of West India Quay station.

A B90 vehicle descending the viaduct from North Quay Junction towards West Ferry. The original London & Blackwall structure is visible, while the new single-track flyover shows the later construction standards.

The Isle of Dogs route

Above **Canary Wharf station while under construction, seen from inside a P89 train at Heron Quays running towards Stratford.**

The route through the Isle of Dogs to Island Gardens runs from the North Quay junction area on the north side of the former West India Docks system on 1986-built bridges across all three docks of the former system. However, it is no longer easy to appreciate the fact that there are three parallel stretches of water because of the infilling of the dock for the mass of the Canary Wharf commercial, retail and leisure developments. The DLR tracks pass into the visually impressive all-over roof of Canary Wharf station, which now has the look and scale of a major heavy rail facility.

Proceeding southwards to Heron Quays the tracks enter Heron Quays station which remains, at the time of writing, largely in the form developed for the initial £77m railway. Heron Quays itself remains largely undeveloped. It was on this quay, prior to the building of the DLR, that a Dash 7 short take-off and landing aircraft made a single landing and take-off to demonstrate the feasibility of the subsequent London City Airport, based in the Royal Docks.

A snow scene at Millwall Dock with the DLR crossing in the distance.

An entrance to Canary Wharf station from within the complex of buildings it serves.

After crossing the docks the route curves sharply to the east on a typical Light Rail style curve, and descends slightly to the station at South Quay before rising again to cross the Millwall Cut, the narrow section of water linking the former West India Dock System with the Millwall Docks. From here the line continues, still on newly-built viaduct, towards Crossharbour station. Between South Quay and Crossharbour the line curves to the south apparently following the shape of the Harbour Exchange office development, but in fact the railway was erected first, and the offices were designed to follow the DLR alignment. Crossharbour station is located on the south-east side of the London Arena and to the north-west of the Asda store which serves as a district centre.

After Crossharbour the alignment of a disused railway embankment carries the line south beside East Ferry Road to a point where it turns east and crosses the road on a new section of bridge structure which also supports Mudchute station. South of Mudchute the route rejoins the 1872 built single-track viaduct which runs through the south western corner of Millwall Park, reaching Manchester Road. A new bridge section carries the line across Manchester Road to a simple 'V' plan layout terminus with two linked side platforms at Island Gardens. Passengers can cross under the Thames to Greenwich by way of the 1902 pedestrian tunnel.

Above **Crossharbour station with the London Arena behind. This station now has an extended roof structure using the parts made redundant by the rebuilding of South Quay.**

Left **A train approaching Island Gardens platform 1, which has been extended to allow two-vehicle trains. Platform 2 remains a single-vehicle platform.**

The Stratford route

Above **The viaduct between North Quay Junction and Poplar station includes the longest span bridge on the DLR. This view shows two trains of P89 stock on the Stratford service.**

The line to Stratford heads east from the North Quay junction area and descends to Poplar station. The Operations and Maintenance Centre is on the northern side of the railway. It is in the Poplar area that the tightest curves on the system are to be found, around 40 metres. Leaving Poplar the line descends to ground level and then turns northwards into a shallow cutting towards All Saints station along a former BR railway alignment. Alongside All Saints station two sidings have recently been provided for vehicle storage. Between All Saints and Devons Road station the line runs either slightly below ground level or at grade. Nearby features consist of old-established council flats to the east of the line and small-scale factory units on the western side. The line crosses the Limehouse Cut Canal at a point where a former Spratts dog biscuit factory has been converted into residential units away from the Thames riverside. The wooden fencing here assists in noise reduction. East of Devons Road station a partly-completed new industrial park has been built on the former British Rail Devons Road motive power depot. Approaching Bow Church station the line runs through a rectangular concrete tunnel which forms the base of residential units built by the Greater London Council when this alignment was still carrying freight traffic to the docks.

North of Bow Church the railway is reduced to a single track and a new climbing curve carries this track from the former North London Railway alignment up to the embankment of the relatively little used British Rail link between Fenchurch Street and Stratford. This latter line merges with the tracks of the Liverpool Street to Stratford multiple track alignment, with the single track DLR route simply located on the extreme south side of the embankment. This part of the route is surrounded by an industrial environment but as the train approaches Stratford there is already some evidence of commercial regeneration with new office blocks built near the commercial centre of Stratford. At Stratford, a bay platform never used by intended BR services to Fenchurch Street was available at the western end of Stratford's up platforms and this ultra-simple terminus arrangement is used by DLR trains. Passengers can change to British Rail services and London Underground's Central Line at the same level as well as to the low-level station platforms where North London Link services call.

Bow Church station on the Stratford line has seen development around it, with new apartments in the background. It remains much as originally built but now has extended platforms.

The Stratford end of the DLR, where a single platform face neighbours BR and London Underground lines. Most of the line between here and Bow Church is single track, with a passing loop at Pudding Mill Lane.

The Beckton route

A train at Beckton Park, one of two stations on the Beckton line built within and below roundabouts on the Royal Albert Dock Spine Road.

Like the Stratford route the Beckton extension begins at the complex of tracks now in place at North Quay junction and serves Poplar station using the most northerly and southerly of the four tracks at this station; the north side track is the Down Beckton and the south side track is the Up Beckton. The Down Beckton flies over the Stratford tracks at the eastern end of the Operations and Maintenance Centre and continues as an elevated railway over Preston's Road and through the Leamouth area, an area currently still being redeveloped.

South of the alignment the remains of the former Brunswick Wharf power station, itself built on the site of the original London and Blackwall terminus can be seen. The first station on the extension, called Blackwall, is located east of Preston's Road and East India station south of the Aspen Way–Lower Lea Crossing road.

The line then proceeds north-eastwards around the convoluted bends of the River Lee on its final approach to the River Thames. A station is under construction at Canning Town, parallel to the A1011 Silvertown Way but on a site that is to be substantially altered to accommodate the authorised Jubilee Line Extension platforms, new platforms for the BR service to North Woolwich and a bus station. The Beckton line opened without Canning Town station.

A train heads towards Beckton from East India station passing the remaining part of Brunswick Wharf Power Station.

The Beckton line has been built into the narrow strip between the River Lea and the A13 road at the western approach to Canning Town.

The western approach to Royal Victoria station on the Beckton line. The space to the left of the DLR station is for a future possible station on the North London link.

A Beckton-bound train leaves Prince Regent. The level section of viaduct in the background is the site of the proposed Connaught station.

The line to Beckton then parallels the Railtrack line southwards then eastwards into the Royal Docks area. A future stop is planned at Thames Wharf, then the line heads east with stations called Royal Victoria, Custom House, and Prince Regent along the line which is effectively at grade here on the south side of Victoria Dock Road. A future stop is planned near the Connaught Crossing road bridge. East of this road bridge there are three further stations at Royal Albert, Beckton Park and Cyprus with the alignment running on the north side of the Royal Albert Dock and parallel to it. Along this section the line is located in the centre-line of the dual carriageway Royal Albert Dock Spine Road. The stations at Beckton Park and Cyprus are built at ground level in the centre of roundabouts with pedestrian links north and south. Footbridges will take passengers under the road, but over the railway: they are known as bowl stations.

After Cyprus station the line turns northwards after first curving southwards of the large roundabout at the junction of the east-west and north-south road network at the eastern end of the Royal Docks system. The next station is at Gallions Reach immediately to the west of the alignment of the planned East London River Crossing road bridge. The Beckton depot is further to the east of Gallions Reach and will, once the road bridge is in place, be visually separated by the northern approach roads.

The line then curves north westwards, to terminate at Beckton, near the existing junction of Tollgate Road and East Ham Manor Way, to the east of the existing Asda District Centre.

The Beckton line in the central divide of the Royal Albert Dock Spine Road looking eastwards to Cyprus station.

Aerial view of Beckton Park station.

Station facilities

Even though the original plans for the railway were based around using Light Rail technology, little of the ultra-simplicity of typical European Light Rail has been incorporated into DLR station design.

Whereas low platforms (with or without ramp access to cars) and bus type shelters are typical of even new systems, the DLR design consultants evolved by 1984 a more sophisticated package incorporating high level traditional British platforms, lifts and lift towers, and high arched platform canopies. The design of the stops also inevitably grew visually once the elevated route had been adopted, particularly where all-new construction was envisaged on the Isle of Dogs; it was helpful to the image to have the station structures on view.

However, in one important respect the stations remained simple and cheap to operate and that was in the decision to leave them unstaffed, relying instead on closed-circuit television (CCTV), spot-checks and a frequent train service to provide inspection. This policy led to considerable local apprehension, led by Island residents' groups and the Docklands Forum, an active pressure group. However, not only have the stations remained remarkably safe for passengers but the incidence of graffiti and vandalism has not been the great curse that it was predicted to be.

However, the elevated location of most of the original stations has been a cause of justifiable complaint when passengers have been exposed to strong winds blowing across the expanses of nearby water. The balance of facilities was probably about right in relation to the proposed frequency of service and budget of the original railway. Even so, in respect of disabled access, the provision of 29 disabled lifts, giving access for wheelchairs, those carrying children and/or heavy shopping to each platform, combined with only a three-inch (75mm) gap between platform edge and the car entrances, meant that a real improvement in access standards was achieved. Again, there have been criticisms: the lift towers and lifts themselves could have had windows fitted to aid a sense of wellbeing and to reduce any feelings of isolation (this feature has been incorporated in the lifts on the Beckton extension). Secondly, the bases of the lift towers have sometimes had to be located away from the threshold of the stairs. Unfortunately this has been a product of geometry, for if the lift doors and stairs are close by at platform level they cannot always be close by at ground level given that lifts rise vertically and stairs descend diagonally.

As set out in the original contract of 1984, sixteen stations were to have been provided. In the event the original Canary Wharf station never opened (but was inspected by some visitors prior to the public opening in August 1987) and was dismantled as a preliminary to the upgrading work carried out by GEC-Mowlem. Even so, 15 stations in place on only 7.5 miles of route gave good access to the system.

The station design at Heron Quays had been developed in the early days as the prototype kit of parts of canopies, lifts and distinctive railings. It remains largely unchanged today.

Opposite **The Beckton line stations feature curved glass structures supported on tubular steel columns, providing light and airy passenger areas.**

Station design

Bank – The only tube-tunnel station on the DLR, Bank has two platforms with a single turnback siding to the west of it. It is reached via a rebuilt Bank/Monument station concourse which permits interchange with the Central, Northern, Circle and District lines.

Tower Gateway – The original City terminus is unlike any of the other stations. L-shaped in plan and elevated, its original entrance was approached via a glass rotunda at the foot of the DLR's original two escalators (plus a stairway). A second exit at the eastern end of the island platform was opened in 1990 and an additional staircase added at the west end alongside the original ones.

Shadwell – An island platform design squeezed on to the existing viaduct where two Railtrack and two DLR tracks are accommodated. It has a single lift at the western end with access at ground level near Watney Street.

Above and left **Tower Gateway**, the original City terminus, uses on a larger scale some of the design elements found at other stations on the railway as first built.

Westferry station. The skyline in the background has completely transformed since the railway was opened.

Limehouse – Is similar in principle to Heron Quays at platform level but has been designed to fit around the 1840-era brick arch viaduct beside the Railtrack Limehouse station.

Westferry – Is unusual in having the platforms straddling the street on an overbridge (over Limehouse Causeway). There are two separate mini-concourse areas at ground level, one on the north side of the street and the other on the south.

Poplar – As built, this station featured three tracks serving two island platforms with two western-end located lifts, similar to the arrangement at Shadwell. Rebuilding has occurred in connection with the Beckton extension to provide a four-track, two island platform layout — the two outer tracks for Bank to Beckton services. An overhead bridge links the platforms to both Poplar High Street and the other side of Aspen Way.

The rebuilt platforms at the enlarged Poplar station, with a B90 stock train on the Stratford service.

Poplar station entrance and footbridge over the tracks and the parallel Aspen Way.

Lamp standards stand to attention on Poplar platforms with the original Operations and Maintenance Centre in the background.

For the benefit of passengers at the front of trains, station names on the Beckton line are displayed at the end of the platform facing the direction of travel.

Blackwall – Is a simple viaduct station with side platforms. Access from the ground level concourse and ticket area is by staircase and lift. An adjacent bus station will be provided for interchange and pedestrian walkways will link with nearby developments.

East India – Is unusual in that it is on three levels with the concourse at mezzanine level and platforms at high level. A footbridge across the adjacent dual carriageway links a major development to the north, directly into the concourse and escalators are provided from here to the two side platforms. Provision has been made for another major development to the south of the station.

Canning Town – Will eventually form an interchange with the present North London Railway's service and the Jubilee Line Extension. The station will be on three levels with elevated DLR tracks, ground level for the other services and a sub-surface concourse. There will also be a major bus station.

Royal Victoria – Is a simple ground level station with side platforms. A bridge served by stairs and lifts, and with provision for future escalators, provides access between platforms and across the adjacent North London Line.

Custom House – Is another ground level station, this time with an island platform. Interchange is provided with the BR Custom House station by way of a footbridge which directly serves both BR platforms, as well as the DLR services.

East India has an escalator up to each platform in addition to the standard lifts. There is also a third lift from intermediate level to street level.

For security, closed circuit television cameras are installed at stations, transmitting pictures via land lines alongside the track to the Control Centre.

Lifts on the Beckton line are conspicuous by their red towers. This view also shows the new standard design of station sign and the circular housing for the ticket issuing equipment.

Prince Regent – Is at the beginning of the Connaught Viaduct and is slightly elevated. The adjacent proposed Londondome development gives the probability of high peak passenger flows, and the single island platform and staircases are wider than normal. A wide high level walkway links the station with a proposed future bus station on Victoria Dock Road and provides for a future link into Londondome.

Royal Albert – Is a simple viaduct station with side platforms. Access to the platforms from the ground level concourse is by lifts and stairs, although there is provision for future escalators.

Beckton Park and **Cyprus** – Are of identical design. In this area the
DLR runs in the centre reserve of the Royal Albert Docks Spine Road
and these two stations are built under elevated roundabouts.
Entrance to the stations is from adjacent residential streets,
underneath the roundabout. A footbridge provides level access to the
other side of the DLR with a short staircase and ramps leading down
to the two side platforms.

Gallions Reach – Is identical to Royal Albert.

Beckton – Is a simple centre platform terminus station with a short
staircase and ramp leading down from the end of the platform to the
adjacent street. Ticket machines and staff amenities are on the
platform.

Beckton Park, one of the
two bowl stations.

The terminus at
Beckton.

Below Devons Road station on the Stratford line. Visible are the simple street level structures provided here and at neighbouring Bow Church station. A ticket issuing point is flanked by the two lift towers.

Opposite Neighbouring stations at the top of the section to Island Gardens are West India Quay and the grand structure within the Canary Wharf commercial development. The westernmost track visible in the upper photograph leads to the system's tightest curve (40 metres) in passenger use as it negotiates North Quay junction.

Stratford – Remains largely as built, but with a slightly extended waiting area. DLR trains terminate in the previously unused bay platform number 4. At platform level the lift is located at the extreme opposite end of the station, necessitating travel along the full length of the island platform.

Bow Church and **Devons Road** – At each of these stations, the road-level open concourse leads down to platforms via separate side staircases.

All Saints – Similar to Bow Church and Devons Road except that the east side platform is located slightly further south than that on the west side.

Poplar – As described under the Bank to Beckton route. Trains from Stratford use the two centre tracks.

West India Quay – As built and used, this was based on the Heron Quays model. The station closed in late 1991 in order to allow the southern approach to the North Quay junctions to be remodelled. West India Quay now features two island platforms with four faces after reopening on 28th June 1993.

Canary Wharf – As built was based on the Heron Quays model but was dismantled and replaced by the present three track, six platform face design incorporating two island platforms and two side platforms. Its distinctive overall roof and escalator provision give it a definite 'big railway' image.

Heron Quays – As role model this remains largely unaltered except for the lengthening of its platforms carried out as part of the upgrading works, and an interconnecting walkway underneath the railway, now removed.

South Quay – Similar to Heron Quays as originally built. The extension to double length resulted in slightly offset platforms. The very heavy usage of this station has required extensive rebuilding of stairways on safety grounds. Full length platform canopies have also been provided. This work started in January 1994 and the station remained open throughout.

Crossharbour – Similar at platform level to Heron Quays but variations in local ground level have resulted in a more complicated arrangement of stair and access ramps. The old canopies from South Quay have been used to add to those originally provided.

Mudchute – Similar to Heron Quays.

Island Gardens – Another one-off, featuring an elevated two-platform V-shaped layout, one platform has been extended to permit double length trains. The reinforced concrete structure was finished with false brick arches using old stock bricks. One arch was modified to accept the DLR shop. An additional staircase was added in 1992.

Above **Original design of station name sign.**

Opposite **Heron Quays, the prototype for the Initial Railway.**

Below **Island Gardens station, where platform 1 on the left has been extended.**

Fares and tickets

The DLR fare structure follows the London zonal fare system beginning in Zone 1 at Bank and Tower Gateway, through Zone 2 for the majority of its stations to Stratford which is in Zone 3. The Beckton line extends to Zone 4. Initially a method of using locally purchased tickets varied from the London norm by requiring a two-step approach: first the purchase of a ticket from multi-destination machines and then its single validation in a separate validator immediately before travelling on the railway.

Although the DLR sought to establish a strong local identity this has, to an extent, clashed with passengers' awareness of the acceptance of standard Travelcards issued at other railway stations as such tickets do not require validation in DLR station validators. This was initially a cause of some confusion to passengers. In every case, passengers entering DLR stations and crossing the red line painted at station thresholds, are required to have a valid ticket.

Above left A ticket issuing machine on DLR.

Above right Bank station showing the red line that defines the boundary of the fare-paid area on all DLR stations. Inability to present a valid ticket inside this area renders a person liable to a penalty.

Earlier 1986-era plans to sell DLR tickets in multiple in packets at such outlets as Building Society premises for later validation were not proceeded with. Currently DLR machine-issued tickets are compatible with London Underground's ticketing system for journeys through to London Underground stations and are also valid to certain British Rail destinations in Essex. A 'Docklander' ticket is available giving unlimited travel for one day on the DLR.

The original ticket equipment consisted of Tollpoint ticket machines and Travelog ticket validators supplied by Thorn-EMI Electronics, Wells, Somerset. Unlike certain Swiss/German validators the DLR type did not cut off any part of the DLR ticket to validate it; rather tickets were absorbed completely into the validator, read and returned in seconds to the traveller. Given that no other remote ticket outlets were selling DLR type tickets, it was found possible and desirable to dispense with separate validation completely. Ticket machines were converted to issue ready-validated tickets at Tower Gateway on 5th June 1989 and elsewhere on the railway seven days later. New Westinghouse machines installed in 1991 at Tower Gateway and Canary Wharf take £5 and £10 notes.

Railway headquarters and offices

Planned as a local operation, the DLR developed with its own physically separate headquarters and train depot, referred to as the Operations and Maintenance Centre. The OMC came into use at the beginning of 1987 and has since been extended in a number of ways to try to accommodate the growing business. (Located in Poplar, on former railway land south of Poplar High Street, the original OMC consists of a steel framed building on piled foundations with offices at the western end and a three track workshop to the east). The original stabling sidings on the north side of this structure have been twice increased in number, initially close to the OMC but more recently on spare land parallel to the running lines south of All Saints Church. New office structures have been built on the other side of the OMC site and the rebuilding of Poplar Station on the Beckton route flyover alignments have further impacted on what has become a fully utilised and busy base.

Poplar OMC with the New Control Centre and footbridge connection to the original control facility, photographed from Canary Wharf 50th floor.

Trains in Poplar Depot during the weekend shut-down. The roof line of the P stock (left) can be compared with the B stock

The opportunity has been taken with the Beckton extension to create a new depot site at the extreme eastern end of the line to the east of Gallions Reach station and to the east of the alignment of the future East London River Crossing (ELRC) bridge approach road. This new facility is needed to house and maintain a significant part of the increased fleet. The original concept of the initial railway of 11 vehicles using extensive offsite contractors' maintenance facilities is no longer appropriate. The new Beckton depot is equipped to a standard appropriate for a railway of 70-80 vehicles allowing space for efficient working on maintenance.

The new depot also gives the means of improving the accommodation of maintenance staff to remove the problems of temporary buildings that were needed to keep the railway operational during its period of very fast growth.

Beckton depot has modern wheel turning equipment as well as all other heavy machinery workshops and offices that will give the maintenance staff the ability to increase their productivity as the expanded railway achieves stability.

The OMC site at Poplar will remain both as a central administration base and an operating base needed for flexibility of working. The stabling of trains will continue as will light maintenance. Both the train operating depots have full signalling and these will on achievement of full resignalling be run from their own dedicated control rooms. Poplar control room will also incorporate much improved facilities to regulate the working of train captains.

Opposite **The Beckton Depot building includes a large amount of office space over workshops and has two observation rooms.**

Above **Beckton Depot maintenance building is fronted by track access. The signalling control room is on the left side.**

Inside Beckton Depot half the area is equipped with comprehensive maintenance pits allowing full access to all underframe equipment and bogies.

During the expansion of the railway there has been need for extra accommodation for staff on project management.

The Bank Tunnel had an extensive temporary building, adjacent to the tunnel mouth, which has now been removed. The Beckton Extension works have been administered from a similar temporary site at Canning Town on LDDC land. This site will last longer than originally planned to cater for the DLR works concerned with the Jubilee Line Extension.

In addition the railway has required the services of many consultant staff as well as its own staff to project manage the Beckton Extension and Resignalling contracts. These together with the staff of the Prime Contractor employed to co-ordinate much of the work are housed in leased offices on the Isle of Dogs.

The original concepts of the small control room run essentially by one person have long been proved inadequate to operate the railway. The upgrading and extension work was always behind the passenger flows being demanded and this situation led to the decisions being made to resignal the railway with the intent of improving the throughput of trains. The many other changes to subsidiary systems such major works entail resulted in the best long term solution being a New Control Centre (NCC).

The NCC has been built at Poplar within the site boundary of the OMC. It houses all the systems needed to run the passenger railway and provides a substantially increased size of control room. The control room has space provision for the levels of staff needed and directly adjacent manager's office and personal needs facilities. The new signalling system is controlled from here and the operation has been built up during the testing and commissioning of the Beckton extension. As the existing railway is transferred to the new systems, its operation will also be from the NCC, leading to a railway fully fit to enter the 21st Century.

Inside the new Control Centre, staff operate all the equipment to supervise the operations. Here the closed circuit television monitors show stations on the Beckton line; the Public Address console is in the foreground.

Signalling and train control initially

The first premise of the Initial Railway signalling and train control was that all the equipment must have been in use on other railways before the designs could be accepted by DLR. Thus the successful contracting group GEC-Mowlem installed a signalling system drawing heavily on the already established British Rail Solid State Interlocking (SSI). Instead of visible signals on the lineside the use of systems of track-to-train tone transmission allowed each train to be controlled safely and manually driven safely. The system of fixed block signalling was the basis of keeping trains a safe distance apart. The use of train carried micro-computers meant that the speed/distance running information could be stored on each vehicle's ATO system. This was largely adequate for the Initial Railway with its small fleet of trains not able to work in multiple unit for public service.

The upgrading of the railway needed more of the same by reducing block length and installing more equipment at the trackside and on more trains. The extension of service to 2-unit trains was designed to allow single-unit trains the flexibility of continuing to stop nearest the platform entry/exit place. This immensely complicated the ATO needs but the P89 trains achieved it after midnight oil was burnt by contractors' engineers. Later the same lessons were learnt by the different ATO contractor for the B90 vehicles and they too became reliable.

On top of all this equipment of track and trains a system of Automatic Train Supervision (ATS) was produced to automate as much as possible the service running of trains and display information to operators in the control room at the OMC. As the railway settled down and services were varied to meet significantly rising demand, the restrictions of fixed block working and a system which was essentially unidirectional began to be realised. For the Beckton extension an opportunity was presented to re-think and see if a financial case was available to change to something with higher flexibility.

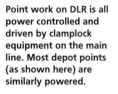

Point work on DLR is all power controlled and driven by clamplock equipment on the main line. Most depot points (as shown here) are similarly powered.

Resignalling

Late in 1989 and in early 1990 a performance specification was assembled for contractors to bid to for full resignalling of DLR. The specification had to allow any system to be supplied but still retained the basic premise that no significantly new systems would be considered.

At the conclusion of bidding two companies survived to be fully evaluated. One offered a system based on traditional fixed block with many additions. The other was offering the concept of moving block which was already in service in Canada and potentially offered higher capacity of working.

Thus in May 1990 the Alcatel company from its Canadian SEL division received a contract to resignal the railway and had the benefit of providing the original equipment of the Beckton branch as a test track.

The basis of the resignalling scheme is a system of moving block with full bidirectional working on all tracks. This centres on the system called SELTRAC and consists of a central control system continuously communicating with all vehicles within the control area. The control area is divided up into sections each approximately 6.25m long and the trains can be followed by the central control to this level of accuracy. The system takes account of the circumstances surrounding each train and instructs each train what it should do. As a result the trains can run closer together and the capacity of the railway is thereby increased.

The operational modes of the trains have been designed to carry on the original system's flexibility with both automatic and manually driven modes controlled and protected by SELTRAC as well as the restricted emergency shunt mode for depot running or mainline recovery from failure. With SELTRAC any vehicle in a train can be in control, which will provide DLR with much needed improved reliability of public service with two-vehicle trains.

The system design caters for three-vehicle trains should this ever be considered in the future.

The principal mechanism used as a back up for SELTRAC is a system of fixed block train tracking using axle counters. This enables trains to be followed and points locked without the use of any track circuits. This allows for a much simpler arrangement of connections to the rails and easy installation on the original railway. As a back-up system DLR are able to move trains at low speed to keep passengers moving on their journeys. The Beckton extension opened on Monday 28th March 1994 with a service to Poplar using platform 4 as a temporary terminus. The initial service run is a three-train 13-minute interval off-peak and a five-train 10-minute interval peak pattern.

The progress of resignalling the Initial Railway routes is well underway with most equipment installed. Testing takes place outside traffic hours to prove items not used for Beckton. There are two more Vehicle Control Centres involved with this task and demonstrating they all work together is complicated. The complexity of the North Quay/Poplar area has necessitated many weekends of test.

Power supply and permanent way

Traction current is distributed at 750V dc by means of an I-section aluminium conductor rail with a stainless steel contact surface bonded to the underside. This conductor rail is of the bottom contact type with an inverted U-section plastic shroud fitted over the top. This helps to minimise the risk of accidental electrocution and avoids the problem of snow and ice build-up associated with low-level current collection systems.

The DLR train cars are fitted with copper collection shoes mounted on glass reinforced plastic arms, centrally-mounted on each side of the motor bogies. A possible future change may see the copper shoes on the cars replaced with a carbon collector, which has recognised long-life qualities and which can help to suppress electric arcing which can aggravate conductor rail wear at the ends of sections.

DLR permanent way is standardised on the use of BS80A 80lb per yard flat bottom rail laid on a mixture of ballasted and concrete trackbed forms. The Pandrol 'e' clip fastening is used on British Rail F24 type sleepers for ballasted track and a cast iron baseplate assembly on slab track. New structures and all curves of less than 100 metres radius are based on the formed concrete trackbed; other sections using traditional railway ballasting. Continuous welded rail is used throughout with alumino-thermic welds.

For the Beckton line considerable lengths of the viaduct are a trough section with ballasted track forms used within the trough. This greatly reduces the noise reflecting off the trackbed and reverberations of the structures. Concrete deck trackbed is used elsewhere with direct fixings. The ground level track is normal ballasted construction. All track is BS80A and no track mounted lubrication is fitted.

Cross-sections of running and conductor rails

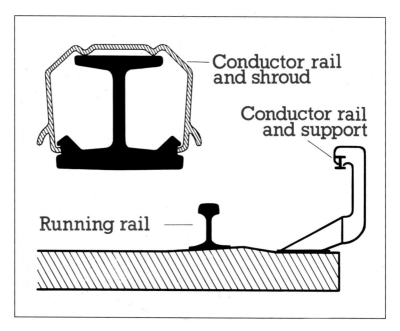

Conductor rail and shroud

Conductor rail and support

Running rail

Staffing

Although the brand-new DLR gave its embrionic management team the chance to create fresh, modern staffing conditions, the smallness of the initial system brought the problem of the diseconomies of small scale.

Roughly 100 jobs were advertised in the period before opening in 1987, with over 2,200 applicants chasing the initial 54 traffic jobs. In the event, half of the successful traffic job applicants lived in the immediate Docklands area and the remainder in East London.

DLR was determined to use the benefit of automation to use staff to humanise the railway. Free from the need to drive trains staff could meet the customers, check tickets, and exert a presence in a variety of ways to oversee and aid the general running of the railway.

The formal title of the Train Captains is Traffic Assistant, because their working brief is broader than the obvious duties on DLR trains: station-based ticket inspection and passenger supervision, train fault finding and inspection, off-the-railway local community PR work and other tasks are all undertaken. This in-built flexibility is considered to have served the railway well with the basic role developing into one providing station staffing at Bank, Tower Gateway and Canary Wharf as necessary.

Maintenance staff, understandably, have their backgrounds more firmly in railways, with many having come from the Underground or British Rail. Additionally, a variety of design, development and project management roles have been created to manage the various separate contracts whilst keeping the original railway open for business as much as possible.

There are currently 130 Traffic Assistants. The total size of the workforce on completion of the development of the railway is expected to number some 370 people.

A train captain at work.

The train service

The Performance Specification designed for the Initial Railway specified eight trains per hour on the two routes (Tower Gateway to Island Gardens and Stratford to Island Gardens). In fact the railway opened with six trains per hour on each service with testing to full specification taking place in 1987/88 with a view to increasing the service in 1988 to that originally planned.

The initial peak service called for 9 trains operating at 10-minute intervals on each service, and 7 trains in the off-peak every 12 minutes. An enhanced peak service using 10 trains was introduced later in 1988, with intervals of 7½ minutes scheduled on each service. At the same time, the station dwell times were reduced. The off-peak service was also increased to every 10 minutes (9 trains).

With the upgrading of the Initial Railway commencing very soon after its public opening, it became necessary to close down certain sections of line for the engineering work involved and to run buses in place of the trains. This started in May 1988, affecting all routes after 21.30 daily, with sections of closures at weekends prior to 21.30. However, from 11th February 1989 it was decided to close the entire railway at weekends as well as from 21.30 on Mondays to Fridays and this has remained the case to date. There have been certain exceptions to this to meet special events. For example, on 5th July 1989 (an LUL strike day) and 8th July 1989 (Tall Ships event), all eleven P86 trains were in service. In the case of the strike day, additional trips were operated direct between Tower Gateway and Stratford, while on the latter occasion additional trips were run between Tower Gateway and Island Gardens. Other occasions of services continuing to run beyond the normal engineering shut-down period include special events at the London Arena and the London Marathon.

The entry into service of the P89 stock allowed a modest service increase from 5th November 1990, with 13 single-unit trains being scheduled. This saw the peak service improved to 6½-minute intervals, necessitating the regular use of the passing loop at Pudding Mill Lane (between Bow Church and Stratford).

From 25th February 1991, following a long period of testing, two-unit trains were timetabled for the first time. The teething troubles with two-unit operation had not been wholly overcome, however, and single units on two-unit workings continued to operate — and sometimes still do. But the timetable saw the peak-hour services on both branches increased to 5-minute intervals with seven 2-car and eight 1-car trains scheduled on the Tower Gateway–Crossharbour and Stratford–Island Gardens services respectively. This was the first regular use of the new Crossharbour centre reversing siding, where all two-car trains had to reverse, as Mudchute and Island Gardens could still only accommodate one-unit trains. In fact two-unit operation was confined to off-peak periods to start with as the new B90 trains (the first of which had arrived on 31st January 1991) were not then available for passenger service. These had started to come on stream in time for the first stage of the opening to Bank on 29th July 1991 when the Tower Gateway peak service was halved, and alternate trains diverted to operate to and from Bank, also having a 10-minute service.

All trains running to and from Bank used the westbound tunnel on a 'single line' basis initially and thus minimum reversing time was allowed. By now many two-car trains were able to be operated of both P89 and B90 stock (but not of mixed types), and the peak stock requirement was for 7x2 (Bank/Tower Gateway–Crossharbour) and 8x1 (Stratford–Island Gardens). In the off peak period, each service operated every 10 minutes (Bank, Tower Gateway and Stratford), but the eight single units that operated the peak Stratford service were shared between the Stratford and Tower Gateway service, the latter being extended to terminate at Island Gardens because of the shorter trains.

The completion of the eastbound running tunnel and subsequent full opening of the Bank extension on 29th November 1991 called for a total of eight two-unit trains in the peaks, four each on the Tower and Bank services. This enabled each service to be self-contained and the extra train catered for the additional time needed at Bank to reverse in the headshunt west of the station. Total stock requirement was thus 8x2 and 8x1, 16 trains and 24 vehicles. (The proposal to run a five-minute peak service to Bank and no service at peak times to Tower Gateway was dropped at a late stage, and certainly after publicity had been made available announcing the proposal). The off-peak service was the same as hitherto, with the Tower Gateway service operated by single unit trains and extended to Island Gardens.

Although major upgrading work had been proceeding on the Docklands Light Railway from very soon after its opening, Mudchute and Island Gardens stations on the south leg still remained capable of accommodating one unit trains only, a problem being the restricted space at Island Gardens and the possibility of a future extension under the River Thames to Lewisham, which would need new stations anyway. However, it was subsequently decided to lengthen these two stations to take two-unit trains and the quickest option was to close completely for a period of time, from after traffic on Friday 6th March 1992. Because of the restricted space available at Island Gardens, it was only possible to lengthen one platform (No.2), the other being retained for single-unit trains only. The railway reopened on Sunday 12th April 1992, but because of uncompleted work, two-unit trains could still not operate to Island Gardens until June 1992. The timetable introduced on Monday 9th March 1992 changed operating patterns and train formations considerably. This was the first use, on a regular basis, of the centre platforms at Canary Wharf for reversing purposes (where Stratford trains terminated), with Bank trains (two-car) and Tower Gateway (one-car) terminating at Crossharbour. With each service operating at eight-minute intervals, this called for 9x2-car and 6x1-car trains — 15 trains, 24 vehicles). This increased the capacity on the Stratford branch, with a two-unit train every eight minutes (peaks) instead of a one-unit train every five minutes. Both Bank and Tower Gateway gained more frequent services (eight instead of ten minutes), although the latter was effectively reduced by the operation of one-unit trains instead of two. Another change was that the service operated with no reduction during the midday off-peak period.

With the restoration of through services, the principles of the above timetable continued. Requiring one extra unit (10x2 and 5x1 throughout the day — 15 trains, 25 vehicles), the eight-minute pattern on each service continued, although there was a changeover of operating patterns on the peak 'shoulders'.

Further timetable changes were made from 25th January 1993, to match the services provided with the public demand. The peak service remained at eight-minute intervals at the same operating patterns, while that in the off-peak was reduced to ten-minute intervals and evening services (20.00 to 21.30) to every 12 minutes.

Until the original sections of the DLR have been connected to Alcatel signalling, the Beckton service, from its opening on the 28th March 1994, comprises a self-contained shuttle service operating from 05.20 to 21.30 on Mondays to Fridays. Between 07.00 and 19.00, five two-unit trains provide a 10-minute service, and outside these times, three two-unit trains provide a 13-minute service. Only later will a through Beckton to Bank service be possible and at that time all the railway will be controlled through the Alcatel system.

Service changes from summer 1994 are being instituted to create a six-minute interval service from Bank to Island Gardens in the peak period to relieve overcrowding at Bank caused by traffic levels rising each month by 1000 passengers a day.

Heavy use of the service to and from Bank led to an increased frequency from summer 1994.

In contrast, the Beckton end of the line is in the early stages of traffic development.

Local railway history

About three-quarters of the initial DLR system opened in 1987 re-used old railway routes. Some of these older railways had been disused for many years; others remained in service right up to the day the DLR took over the tracks. The origin, development and, in many cases, decay of these railways is closely tied up with the history of the up-river docks.

The City route

In 1836 an Act of Parliament was passed authorising the construction of 'The Commercial Railway' running from Minories, by the City Wall, 3½ miles east to Brunswick Wharf at Blackwall. The railway passed close by the Regents Canal Dock, the West India Docks and the East India Docks. The railway was not initially intended to handle freight — rather it sought to attract large numbers of passengers whose journey from London to the Docks had until then to be made either by river — slow and often circuitous — or by road, which was even slower. Before the introduction of the telegraph, all messages had to be conveyed by hand and a continuous stream of clerks, messenger boys and businessmen travelled to and from the Docks daily. Additionally, the increasing popularity of the seaside had resulted in a growing number of steamer services from London to Kent and Essex resorts — services which could operate far more cheaply and efficiently if they started from Blackwall rather than from the Pool of London.

Two rival schemes had been put before Parliament for very similar routes to the docks and the unsuccessful rivals eventually merged with the Commercial Railway, with George Stephenson and George Bidder becoming the Company's engineers. In 1839, a year after construction had started, the company received parliamentary approval for an extension from Minories to Fenchurch Street and a formal change of name to the London & Blackwall Railway.

Opening on 4th July 1840, the London & Blackwall Railway was in its day a sophisticated and rapid system. Carried mainly on a 4,020-yard viaduct — the cheapest way of building in a congested urban area — the double-tracked railway was cable-hauled using a drum-to-drum system and seven miles of hemp rope for each track, with winding engines at either end of the line.

Within two years of opening the railway had extended into the City to Fenchurch Street and was experimenting with goods traffic. It was however isolated from the rest of the growing London rail network by virtue of its wide track gauge and cable haulage, the cables having a tendency to occasionally twist or snap, despite now being metal instead of hemp. To expand further the railway needed to standardise its equipment. In 1845 Parliament passed an Extension Act for the London & Blackwall Railway, authorising a connection with the Eastern Counties Railway at Bow and the change of gauge and haulage. The last cable-hauled train ran on 14th February 1849.

Poplar to Stratford

The Eastern Counties Railway was incorporated in 1836, to run from Shoreditch to Norwich and Yarmouth. Within the London area the Eastern Counties Railway helped promote and then build the branch line from Stratford to North Woolwich in 1846/7 and had established at Stratford what was to become a major railway works. The London & Blackwall now became part of the growing Eastern Counties network, being eventually leased completely in 1865 to the Eastern Counties Railway, by now termed the Great Eastern Railway.

Other railways besides the Eastern Counties wanted to share in the lucrative docks traffic, and it was through a rival company, the North London Railway, that the DLR section from Bow Church to All Saints came to be built. The North London Railway (NLR) started in 1846 as the East & West India Docks and Birmingham Junction Railway Company. The intention was to build a freight line linking the docks with the London to Birmingham line at Chalk Farm in North London. It took four years to build and open the line as far south as Bow, and it was not until 1851 that the railway reached Poplar. Poplar Dock was served by a large goods depot and an extensive yard of sidings with over 14 miles of track. Part of this area is now occupied by the DLR Operations and Maintenance Centre.

Passing through some of the more prosperous new suburbs of London, the railway company carried passengers from the start, although it was not until 1866 that passenger services extended south of Bow. The heyday of the North London Railway occurred in the last twenty years of the 19th century. Over its Poplar line ran three other major railway companies' freight trains, and around Poplar Docks were grouped huge warehouses.

West India Quay to Island Gardens

In complete contrast to the NLR was the tiny neighbouring Millwall Extension Railway, the route of which is now used by the DLR from Crossharbour to Island Gardens. It began back in 1865 when construction work started on the Millwall Dock. Millwall Dock was built with an internal rail network, designed around horse-hauled wagons — steam locomotives were too much of a fire risk with quaysides of wooden ships, often with canvas sails.

At around the same time, the Great Eastern Railway and the Millwall Canal Company (owners of the Millwall Dock) jointly proposed a railway which would develop the southern part of the Isle of Dogs. Running south from Millwall Junction at the top of the Isle of Dogs, the line would skirt the east side of West India Docks and pass alongside the Millwall Dock to terminate on the bank of the Thames close by the jetty for the ferry to Greenwich.

Although this railway, the Millwall Extension Railway, would benefit its promoters, the neighbouring East & West India Docks saw the line as a threat, abstracting traffic, and they objected vigorously. Thus it was that the Millwall Extension Railway, single track throughout, took six years to build, opening in 1871 to Millwall Docks and in 1872 to North Greenwich station.

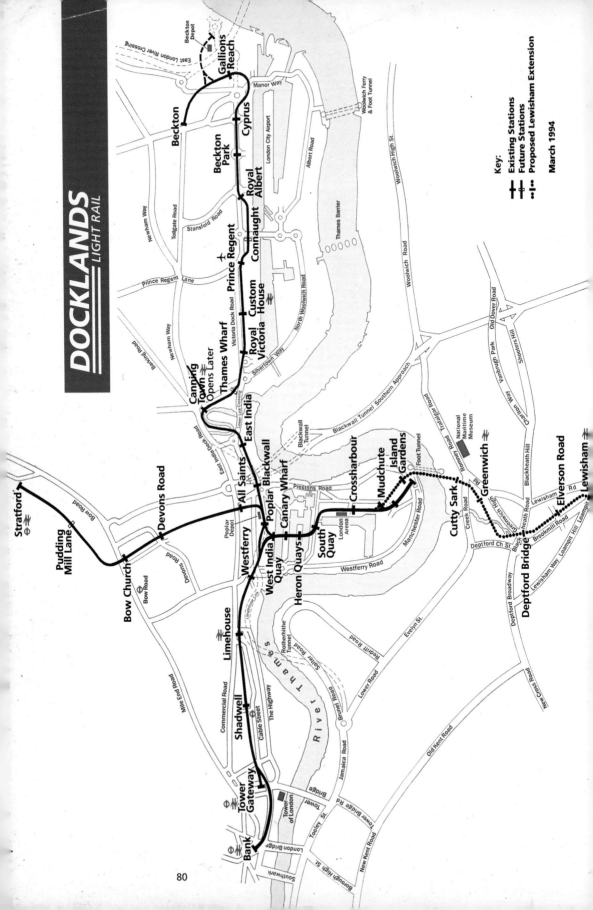

DOCKLANDS LIGHT RAIL

Key:
- Existing Stations
- Future Stations
- Proposed Lewisham Extension

March 1994

Stations and places shown on the map:

Beckton Depot, Gallions Reach, Beckton, Cyprus, Beckton Park, Royal Albert, Connaught, Prince Regent, Custom House, Royal Victoria, Thames Wharf, Canning Town (Opens Later), East India, Blackwall, Poplar, All Saints, Devons Road, Bow Church, Pudding Mill Lane, Stratford, Canary Wharf, West India Quay, Westferry, Limehouse, Shadwell, Tower Gateway, Bank, Heron Quays, South Quay, Crossharbour, Mudchute, Island Gardens, Cutty Sark, Greenwich, Deptford Bridge, Elverson Road, Lewisham

River Thames

London City Airport, Thames Barrier, Woolwich Ferry & Foot Tunnel, National Maritime Museum, Tower of London, London Arena, Poplar Depot

East London River Crossing

Manor Way, Newham Way, Tollgate Road, Stansfeld Road, Prince Regent Lane, Victoria Dock Road, Silvertown Way, North Woolwich Road, Woolwich Road, Woolwich High St, Albert Road, Old Dover Road, Shooters Hill, Vanbrugh Park, Charlton Way, Blackheath Hill, Blackwall Tunnel Southern Approach, Blackwall Tunnel, Preston's Road, Manchester Road, Westferry Road, Banking Road, Newham Way, East India Dock Road, Bow Road, Poplar Road, Devons Road, Mile End Road, Commercial Road, The Highway, Cable Street, Bridge, Tower Bridge Rd, Tooley St, Southwark High St, Borough High St, Jamaica Road, Brunel Road, Rotherhithe Tunnel, Salter Road, Redriff Road, Lower Road, Evelyn St, New Kent Road, Old Kent Road, New Cross Road, Deptford Broadway, Deptford Church St, Creek Road, Greenwich High Rd, Romney Road, Trafalgar Road, Brookmill Road, Lewisham Way, Loampit Hill, Loampit Vale, Lewisham High St, Limehouse Link, Limekiln